With Flowers

A book of poems for infants
chosen by Fred Sedgwick

With flowers	Emily Dickinson	**2**
Journey	Judith Nicholls	**3**
Carnival!	Amryl Johnson	**4**
I've lost my love	Traditional	**6**
How beautiful is the rain	H W Longfellow	**7**
I met an old man by the sea	John Gohorry	**8**
Punky Night	Traditional	**11**
The road is very dirty	Traditional	**12**
A Thinking Christmas	Traditional	**13**
Prayer	Traditional	**14**
Hunky-Dory Daly	Fred Sedgwick	**15**
Good night	Thomas Hood	**16**

Illustrations by:
Maggie Brand p 5; Phillip Burrows p 11; Debbie Clark p 12; Bridget Dowty p 7;
Geraldine Dobbie pp 8–10; Joe Rice p 13; Tessa Richardson-Jones p 2; Felicity Roma
Bowers p 15; Barry Rowe pp 3, 14, 16; Martin Salisbury p 6.

With flowers

I've nothing else to bring, you know,
So I keep bringing these –
Just as the night keeps fetching stars
To our familiar eyes.
Maybe we shouldn't mind them
Unless they didn't come –
Then maybe it would puzzle us
To find our way home.

EMILY DICKINSON

Journey

I am the acorn
that grew the oak
that gave the plank
the Vikings took
to make a boat
to sail them out
across the seas
to England.

JUDITH NICHOLLS

Carnival!

Dance
dance to the steel band
Dance!

Move your body
Enjoy the rhythm

Sing
sing the calypso
Sing!

If you don't know the words
Just hum the tune

Look
look at the costumes
Look!

Bright colours
Every one from a rainbow

Listen
listen to them celebrating
Listen!

Carnival is all about
freedom and joy

Love
love one another
Love!

You have nothing to lose
Be happy together

C - A - R - N - I - V - A - L!

Amryl Johnson

I've lost my love

I've lost my love and I do not care,
I've lost my love and I do not care,
  I'll soon have another
  That's better than the other –
I've lost my love and I do not care.

How beautiful is the rain

How beautiful is the rain!
After the dust and heat,
In the broad and fiery street,
In the narrow lane,
How beautiful is the rain!

How it clatters along the roofs,
Like the tramp of hoofs!
How it gushes and struggles out
From the throat of the overflowing spout!

Across the window pane
It pours and pours;
And swift and wide,
With a muddy tide,
Like a river down the gutter roars.
The rain, the welcome rain!

H W Longfellow

I met an old man by the sea

I met an old man by the sea,
his beard was long and grey;
his coat was torn, his face was worn,
but still he stopped to play.

We played Charades and I-spy,
Hopscotch and Drop-Down-Dead;
I asked him when his birthday was,
and this is what he said:-

'Tuesday the last of Never,
Wednesday the first of When,
Thursday the third of So-I've-heard;
clap hands and ask again!'

We played at Forfeits, Hunt-the-Fish,
Knock-knock and Guess-the-Word;
I asked his birthday once again
and this was what I heard:-

'Sunday the first of Sometimes,
Monday the last of What?
Friday the twelfth of Suit Yourself,
Saturday Mark-the-Spot.'

I asked his birthday one last time;
he rose, and shook his beard;
and this was what he said to me
before he disappeared: –

'Wednesday the ninth of Nothing,
Friday the fifth of Some;
Tuesday the last of Time-was-Past,
Time-Is and Time-to-Come.'

JOHN GOHORRY

Punky Night

It's Punky night tonight,
It's Punky night tonight.
Give us a candle, give us a light
'Cos if you don't you'll get a fright.

It's Punky night tonight,
It's Punky night tonight.
Adam and Eve they wouldn't believe
It's Punky night tonight.

TRADITIONAL

The road is very dirty

The road is very dirty,
My shoes are very clean.

I've got a little pocket
To put a penny in.

If you haven't got a penny,
A ha'penny will do.

If you haven't got a ha'penny
A mince pie will do.

If you haven't got a mince pie
A drink of wine will do.

If you haven't got a drink of wine
God bless you.

TRADITIONAL

A Thinking Christmas

A turkey dinner
at Christmas is great!
>THINK:
>Somewhere. . . . a boy
>with an empty plate

The Christmas tree lights
shine red, green and gold!
>THINK:
>Somewhere. . . . a girl
>shivering and cold

Presents and parties!
Yes, *that's* Christmas Day!
>THINK:
>Somewhere. . . . a babe
>asleep in the hay

WES MAGEE

Prayer

From ghoulies and ghosties
and long-leggedy beasties
and things that go bump in the night

Good Lord deliver us.

TRADITIONAL

Hunky-Dory Daly

My name is Hunky-Dory Daly.
   I ride the weather out.
I see the thunder through the trees
   and hear the lightning shout.

I'm gifted with these useless gifts –
   to smell the bright snowfall,
to taste spring rain on a winter day
   and the cuckoo's call.

My name is Hunky-Dory Daly.
   My gifts I'll give to you
if you will ride the storm with me
   and see the weather through.

FRED SEDGWICK

Good night

Here's a body – there's a bed!
There's a pillow – here's a head!
There's a curtain – here's a light!
There's a puff – and so good night!

THOMAS HOOD